As you heal yourself, you become a healing force in the lives of everyone you know. Since you are one with all things, you actually do unto yourself whatever you do unto others and vice versa. Be kind to everyone, including yourself, and you are healing our world.

HEALING

Key to
Spiritual Balance

Mary Ellen Flora

CDM Publications　　　Everett, Washington

CDM Publications
2402 Summit Ave.
Everett, WA 98201

First Printing 1992

Printed in the United States of America

Library of Congress Catalog Card Number: 92-072953

ISBN 0-9631993-2-3

*This book is dedicated to a healer
of spirit and body:
M. F. "Doc" Slusher*

Table of Contents

List of Illustrations

ACKNOWLEDGEMENTS

Many thanks to Alison Eckels for editing, proofreading, and encouragement. Alison's support and work were invaluable. Thanks also to Reggie Taschereau and Erika Ginnis for proofreading.

I greatly appreciate Bill Broomall's work on all aspects of production and his continuing validation. Also, thanks to Bill for his wonderful song lyrics "God is Moving".

For the art work and supervision of artistic aspects throughout the book many thanks to Gail Coupal. Jeff Gibson's cover photograph is greatly appreciated and admired.

I wish to express my appreciation to the CDM Board of Directors for the financial and spiritual support as well as for their enthusiastic encouragement and advice.

Warmest regards and thanks go to Lewis S. Bostwick who first introduced me to conscious use of spiritual healing techniques.

Greatest appreciation and much love go to M. F. "Doc" Slusher for assisting, encouraging and healing me throughout the project.

God is Moving

Within the dancing stars, the singing sun
Circling in the sky
We see the glories of the wondrous One
    God is moving
    God is with us now
    Changeless changing
    Ever present love
When you feel that you cannot move or change
Turn to the constant clear light
The light that shines into
every dark hidden corner
    God is moving
    Turning turning
    God is with us
    Listen listen
Within the rushing streams of faith and love
Waters of the soul
An ocean cycling full of life and pow'r
    God is moving
    Love into the world
    God is healing
    See the light that grows
Turn your ears to your God
Ask without any fear
Listen and you will hear
Endless wellspring of Love
Life without end
    Like an ocean
    God is moving
    Ever present
    Listen listen

--Bill Broomall

HEALING

Key to
Spiritual Balance

INTRODUCTION

All of us have the ability to heal ourselves. Unfortunately, most people do not realize that they have this ability and the power to heal themselves. Actually, all healing is basically self healing. All that is necessary is for the individual soul to desire healing and believe he can have it.

Most people believe that someone else can heal them and that they cannot do it themselves. This makes people look outside themselves to find healing. When this external focus is chosen, the individual forgets her own healing power and the desired healing cannot occur.

When you look within for your spiritual information, the healing idea forms and the necessary belief or faith emerges. Then you open to the healing energies that are always available within and around you. While you are the one who creates the healing, you do not have to be alone in your healing process. Someone else can assist you in the healing process by being a catalyst or energy booster. In fact, part of the healing process can be attracting the other souls you select to assist in your healing. You choose any helpers you wish or need; then it is part of your healing to let yourself receive the assistance.

The world is full of healers. In fact we all have this ability even if we have allowed it to become dormant. There are many healing arts such as spiritual healing, dentistry, midwifery, medicine, massage, herbal healing, acupuncture, chiropractic and more. The people who have chosen to devote their lives to healing make themselves available to be used in one's healing process. Healers can be found in any of the healing arts. Those who are called to serve others as healers often find themselves involved actively in a healing focus. However, healers can be found everywhere and are not necessarily involved in one of the healing arts. We can find a healer in ourselves if we just allow the healing energy to flow.

Regardless of which healing art or healer you choose to assist you, it is you who actually heal yourself. For example, you may go to a doctor to set a broken bone for you, but you are the one who generates the energy to heal the break. If you go to a psychic healer, he or she may help you remove energy from your body that has been causing pain, but you are the one who generates the faith to make it happen and who keeps the system clear. No matter what healing path you take or what healing helpers you choose, you are the one who discovers what you need and whom to turn to as a catalyst. The information is within you. The assistance is always there waiting for you to discover it.

Over the years, I have seen many people change from having an outward focus to having an inward healing perspective. They change from spiritual children to spiritual adults; from wanting someone to do it for them, to enjoying their ability to heal themselves. I have also seen people refuse to mature and turn within and heal themselves.

I attempted to assist one young man who intellectually knew all the right answers. Unfortunately, he refused to turn within to himself, the spiritual being, and change what was out of balance within himself. He just kept on looking for an easy way out of his dilemma or for someone else to take responsibility for him. He went from one healer to another, both spiritual and physical healers, seeking one who would heal him. He refused to listen to any of them, and at the same time tried all of the healing suggestions on a surface level. His body finally took control of the situation and his physical pain forced him into surgery. Not long after the surgery he recreated the identical problem. He had removed the physical problem, not the spiritual one, thus he was still creating the difficulty in order to force himself to focus within. As far as I know he is still seeking answers to his problems everywhere except within himself.

A woman I know did the opposite of the young man. She knew that she had cancer. In her search for a solution to her problem, she became a member of a group dedicated to spiritual awareness and healing. She learned all of the spiritual techniques to assist her to turn within. She discovered things that she did not like about herself, yet she persevered in her healing. She discovered forgotten painful childhood experiences that caused her to feel intense fear. The emotional response to her abuse experiences had become a disease in her body. Once she worked through the intense emotions that emerged as she remembered, she began to cleanse the destructive energies. Within a year she was informed by her doctor that the cancer was no longer present in her system. This woman has gone on to help others in their healing process, as she continues to heal herself.

The man chose the seemingly easy road of not taking responsibility for his creation. He looked outside himself for his answers, and protected himself from his pain by intellectualizing the information he received. He hid in the darkness that he had created. The woman dug into her dark and disturbing creations and brought them into the light to heal herself. Healing requires that you face yourself and your creations and shine light on them. If you do not face yourself and your creations, you will repeat the same lessons until you learn from them.

Another woman I assisted had an abusive childhood that would not even be detailed on television. The physical circumstances were horrible, yet she was able to regain her spiritual perspective and use her psychic abilities to heal herself of these traumatic emotional and physical experiences.

One of the emotions she had to deal with in herself was hate. As she cleared this vibration from her body her life began to change. Her old friends no longer liked her as they were still filled with this energy and she was not. She found new friends who had fun and were loving. She got a new job and reconciled her relationship with her daughter. By forgiving those in her past she healed herself. She let go of the past so she could create what she wanted in the present. As she changed internally, her external world changed with her. When she was filled with hate, then hate was all around her. When she cleansed the hate from herself, she was free from its overwhelming presence in her life.

These examples are extreme physical manifestations of spiritual problems. Most of us create less dramatic circumstances; yet our pains, stresses, diseases and upsets are just as disturbing to our lives as these extreme examples are to those who created them. We all need healing skills to maneuver successfully through the maze of life. We all need the healing flow from God to solve our problems and cure our ills.

A friend of mine has created heart disease to learn a lesson about receiving. She has spent her life giving to everyone. Her healing skills are so strong and yet so outwardly focused that she created a need to receive in order to do so. By placing herself in a position where she physically has to accept help from others, she is creating the needed change. As she receives, she balances her energy and learns her lesson. Her disease is actually a spiritual healing for her, even though it would not appear so from a physical perspective.

My husband is another example of someone who created a physical illness to heal himself. He was a dentist for twenty years during which time he became allergic to tooth dust. He fought this allergy for several years while still trying to remain in dentistry. Finally he was forced to give up dentistry and he became an orchardist, growing apples. During this time he discovered his spiritual calling as a psychic healer and teacher. He would have had difficulty leaving the healing profession of dentistry for this new focus, but he was already free of that path. Thus he was able to create an organization to help others find and follow their own spiritual path.

I was director of a summer camp for boys with Muscular Dystrophy and Cerebral Palsy. These young men ages six to sixteen taught me a great deal about healing. They lived fully, laughed a lot and enjoyed each day. Even though they were confined to wheelchairs and needed assistance with things we take for granted, they were full of life and wise beyond their years. Many of these young men saw beyond the limits of their bodies and learned to live as the bright lights they are. Some of them were consciously aware they created their illness to spiritually heal themselves and others. We can all transcend whatever we have created in the body to learn from and let ourselves shine to teach others. When we operate as spirit we heal ourselves and others, just as these young men have.

I experienced recurring pain in my head for years. For some time I looked outside of myself, hoping to find an external cause for the pain or at least someone else to blame for it. After no success in this direction, I looked within and discovered the pain was from a childhood injury. As I faced the injury and all that it meant to me spiritually, I cleared the old pain. The techniques that I use, and teach others to use, I share with you in this book.

As I heal myself and watch other people heal themselves, I never cease to be amazed at the healing power available to everyone. Each person I have mentioned did the healing in his or her own way. Each changed his own perspective by clearing energy blocks, learning to know self and by turning within to God. The healers freed themselves by forgiving and letting go. By changing the internal spiritual reality they healed the external physical one. Each one turned within, found his spiritual information and used this spiritual power to heal himself.

I have seen people turn from frightened, hateful people to happy, loving ones. I have seen people overcome their physical pain and fear to become loving and giving. I have also seen those who refuse to heal and remain in the darkness and loneliness of doubt. I could fill a book with the individual stories of healing. Instead, their legacy is this book of healing techniques and inspiration. Hopefully this information will assist many others to heal themselves.

Healing is change. You have the healing power to change anything in your life. Once you have the idea of healing and the belief in it, your healing process happens. The way to get in touch with this healing energy is to turn within and open yourself to the healing flow. Allow the techniques to help you tune in to your spiritual self and your God from whom all healing flows.

Healing is the ability to change our energies and create equilibrium. Healing is how we balance the body to function as the creative communication system it is meant to be.

HEALING

Healing is a gift from God. All energy and all life flow from the Creator; thus all healing ultimately flows from God. To tap into this healing flow you only need to desire it and believe in it. What we believe is what we create. Thus healing is based on belief. The healing concepts presented here are based on the following beliefs: everyone is spirit and a part of God; healing is change; all healing is self healing; and, we create our physical reality from our beliefs.

Each soul creates his experience here on Earth according to what he needs to learn. This schoolhouse format of planet Earth requires that each soul know how to heal himself in order to learn his lessons. Each soul is unique; thus each lesson and each healing process is also unique. As spirit, we reincarnate in many bodies to have the opportunity to learn and grow spiritually. Spiritual growth is a process of continuous healing and change.

HEALING

Healing is a spiritual phenomenon which manifests in the physical realm. Physical illness can be a part of a healing process to regain balance, or it can be an indication that some aspect of self is out of balance. Illness can even be part of an agreement with another soul. The individual soul needs to turn inward to self and God within to discover the path to self healing. Self-knowledge leads to healing; thus one needs to know one's own lessons in order to create healing.

You create your reality with your beliefs, so faith in the healing process is another necessary ingredient to healing. If you do not believe in the process, whatever it is, it will not work for you. If you have faith in your healing process, you will heal.

Healing is the process of making change. Healing is motion and change; it is not a static state. Schoolhouse Earth offers infinite opportunities to learn. Much of our learning process involves balancing dichotomies or opposites. Balancing these dichotomies creates healing. Whether we are speaking of healing from a spiritual or a physical perspective, the same principles apply. If we are out of balance, we need to change to re-balance.

Health of spirit and body is something everyone seeks, whether they seek it consciously or unconsciously. Healing is a focus of all societies and peoples, regardless of the form it takes. Whether the healing has a spiritual focus or a physical focus, the desired result is the same: the desire to be whole and sound. Individuals, families, groups, societies, nations and the world all need healing skills to maintain a balanced, sound state of being.

Key To Spiritual Balance

Healing means to be whole, not divided. When we are whole instead of fragmented, we are sound or healed. When we are divided, we are only partially ourselves and thus are unbalanced. The result of healing is balance, in which we achieve wholeness. When we are in balance, our physical and spiritual systems work in harmony; we are in charge of the entire spectrum of our reality. This equilibrium gives us the power and ability to make decisions and choices, which we need to make in order to accomplish our goals.

Think of experience in this earthly reality as a teeter-totter. When you are on one end of the teeter-totter, the other end is up in the air; and when you go to that end, the opposite end goes up in the air. If you are on either end of the dichotomy, part of you is "up in the air". Only when you balance are both ends on a level. Then you feel safer, are more in control, and have a clear view. Going up and down and balancing on the teeter-totter of life has no right or wrong connected to it, only learning and growing. We often go back and forth in our learning process in order to arrive at the equilibrium we seek with the dichotomies with which we are working.

Since balance is not static we must constantly change to maintain our equilibrium. Just as the planet is constantly in motion within our solar system to maintain its state of harmony with all other planets, we need to keep our reality in motion to experience harmonious proportion with all that is within and around us. The body is also constantly changing and healing itself as the cells of the body continue to renew and rebuild throughout life. Healing allows motion.

The earthly lessons are composed of dichotomies so we can learn balance. Some of the familiar dichotomies we must learn to harmonize are male and female, good and evil, and spirit and body. We are not here to achieve perfection, but to experience balance. Only when we return to God do we experience perfection, for only God is totally complete and whole. God is the only reality which is perfect. Our return to God is a path of learning, healing, balancing and growing until we mature enough to be one with this Divine experience.

While here on Earth as spirit manifesting in a body, you have to remember that the goal is learning and balance, not perfection. You need to learn to work as spirit through the body without ignoring either. You have to remember your spiritual origin and also accept what you are learning through your body. To accomplish what you came here to do, you must discover what you are here to learn and then begin to balance your life to learn the lesson. You have come into this Earth to learn and grow, not to be perfect. Learning and growing are healing.

We reincarnate into many bodies in different life-times to allow for various experiences. Everyone creates specific lessons for each life, as we cannot learn everything in one session in any school. The lessons may include healing ourselves of an imbalance. A soul could be too giving and need to learn to receive. A soul could need to learn humility, or how to deal with power, or any number of lessons.

You may have come to Earth to learn to be personally responsible. You could be out of balance in trying to take responsibility for everyone except yourself. You probably have created circumstances that forced your attention back on you, such as illness or other attention-getting experiences. You may be a healer who thinks of others first and finally finds yourself feeling resentful for giving everything away. You need to re-balance and turn within to discover and meet your own needs. You may find that some of that external focus is an excuse to avoid something you have created, such as pain. Turning within to heal yourself helps you accept and take responsibility for your creations. This acceptance of self, or taking personal responsibility for your creations, no matter how unpleasant, is your lesson. Learning this will set you free to be yourself. This self healing also makes you a more effective catalyst for the healing of others, as you are clearer and will be more loving with others as you accept yourself.

As spirit in a body, we are always trying to balance to stay on track and healthy. There are many ways that we can get off our track, or spiritual path, and create imbalance. We can become lost in our body's desires or emotions. We can make agreements with others that are not beneficial. We can misuse the body or follow any number of temptations.

Sometimes when we try to balance, we overcompensate and move too far to the opposite side and are unbalanced again, only in the opposite manner. For example, you may be experiencing yourself as very aggressive and try to overcome this. In the process you may become so receptive that you lose your sense of self. The healing process, if you keep going, will eventually bring you to a balanced state where you are both receptive and aggressive as needed.

HEALING

Regardless of the individual's unique life lessons, each soul has two contracts that must be kept in every lifetime: one agreement is with God and the other is with the body. Any other agreements we make with other beings, such as marriage and parenting and so forth, can be changed or even broken. The agreements with God and with the body are for the lifetime. We must take responsibility for the body and what we create through it, as well as for fulfilling our agreement with God. If we honor these two agreements, we are healed. If we ignore either, we get out of balance and need to heal ourselves by re-balancing in order to fulfill our life goals.

Our bodies and the planet are ours through which to create. We have to own and take responsibility for our physical reality in order to operate effectively through it. We need to remember how the body works and how we as spirit create through the body. We also need to remember that we are not the body and that we have to teach the body to accept us. It is necessary to heal our body and get in harmony with our earthly creations in order to use them effectively to accomplish our spiritual purpose.

The body is a wonderful instrument created for your learning experience and for your communication with God. The body informs you of what is occurring in your physical world. If you are not balancing correctly, the body will keep sending you messages until it has your attention. It will eventually become ill or hurt itself, if necessary, to get your attention.

When you are out of balance spiritually, you will create a physical manifestation to help you learn to re-balance. It can take two years or more for a physical illness to manifest from a spiritual problem. For example, you may be unable to receive love. Through the years this could develop into a form of heart disease. Or, you as spirit may be confused about the gender of your body if you have been manifesting through male bodies and then are born in a female body. If you do not accept your body and learn how it works, you could create problems with the female organs and eventually create a hysterectomy. There are many ways you can be confused. You need to learn to know yourself spiritually and physically and then you will know what you need to do to heal yourself.

Some of our seemingly impossible problems can be healed by simply letting go of the past and living in the present. We could be trying to solve a problem which we brought forward from a past life and which we find confusing in the present life. This is true of past pains, whether they were created in this or a previous existence. For example, cancer is sometimes a physical manifestation of hate for someone we have not forgiven. Letting go, or forgiving, is healing. When we hate, we hurt ourselves. When we forgive, we are relieved of the corrosion and are healed.

Mainly, we need to keep our spiritual perspective so we can see and know what is occurring both physically and spiritually. With our neutral spiritual perspective we can learn what the experience is about and how to deal with it. For example, if the body has diarrhea or constipation, it is telling us that it is out of balance and needs a change. This physical manifestation could indicate an imbalance between spirit and body. We might need to pay more attention to our body to re-establish our relationship with it.

Maybe we have allowed life to become so busy we are not eating properly. Or, it could be that we are spiritually changing the body and it is responding by cleansing poisons we have stored in it. We need to pay attention to know the cause so we can heal ourselves.

For every spiritual change that we make there is a corresponding physical reaction. When we change our beliefs, we also change our body and it responds. It may sleep more or less, want more food, become ill or have another reaction. The body is made up of our beliefs, so it changes when we change our beliefs. If we believe that we grow through pain and suffering, the body will be full of pain. When we let go of that lie, we can heal the body of the pain we unnecessarily stored in it. We often misuse our body because we believe and create from a lie. Healing involves learning what is correct for the life's purpose and creating the appropriate beliefs through which to work. Many of our physical problems are caused by not using the body correctly. We often treat our car, pets and everyone else better than we treat our own body. We need to remember it is our temple and treat it as such.

Because the world is overly focused on the physical reality and not on the spiritual, many of our spiritual energies are incorrectly diagnosed as body problems. These misdiagnosed problems are often body responses to spiritual changes or energy flows. An example is the use of a spiritual energy called kundalini energy. When we bring this energy up through the spine, we can experience many body symptoms such as back pain, hot flashes or skin rashes. All of these symptoms cure themselves if we keep moving the kundalini energy, but many people seek a physical explanation. Some healing projects have a spiritual solution and some need physical attention. It is our responsibility as spirit to see what we need and provide it.

We need to be in touch with the body to know what we are creating in our physical world. Emotions are the main way the body communicates with us as spirit. The body uses emotions to tell us what is happening. We need to hear this communication to be able to respond to our body and our earthly creations. When we pay attention and respond, we can heal ourselves before there is a major problem.

As babies, we learn that emotions can be effectively used to communicate with others. We need to remember that emotions are also a powerful way to communicate with ourselves. We need to experience our own emotions to know what is occurring in our body. As spirit, we need to be aware of what is happening in our body to be in control of our physical creativity.

Since you are trained to be tuned into others' emotions instead of relating to your emotions, when you begin to experience your own emotions they may feel overwhelming or unfamiliar. When you have been experiencing other people's emotions more than your own, you have to allow time to learn to know yourself. You must be careful not to judge your emotions as they emerge, as the judgement will stop the flow of communication from your body to you.

Emotions are simply a communication from your body to you. There is no good or bad about an emotion, only communication. Unfortunately most people have been taught value judgements about emotions and these judgements block your healing process. For example, you may believe that your anger is bad, and not realize that the body is sending you a message that it is unhappy with a situation, or frightened and dealing with the situation aggressively. Whatever the emotional message the body is sending, it is your responsibility, as spirit, to deal with it. Each emotional message is different and needs to be responded to individually. The important thing is to be aware that the emotionality of the body is its way of communicating to you, the spiritual being, about what is happening in the physical reality.

When you listen to the emotional message of the body, you are able to respond and heal yourself. If the body is communicating fear, you need to pay attention. It could need a rapid healing to stay safe. The body could be telling you to move it across the road before a car hits it. If there is no immediate threat to the body, it could be communicating another type of disturbance, such as the memory of a past experience or anxiety about a future goal. As spirit, you can cleanse those frightening past experiences or future plans by simply letting them go. Since fear generates hate and hate creates disease in the body, you need to forgive and let go to heal yourself. You can heal any aspect of your experience when you operate as spirit.

Judgement is one of the most limiting views we can have of our emotionality. Judgement keeps us from hearing the message from the body, as we are busy determining if it is good or bad. We miss a great deal of information from this reality by judging, instead of listening and responding constructively. When we judge our emotions, we are blocking the communication from our body and thus not healing ourselves.

For example, when the body is expressing hate, if you judge this emotion you will keep it and bury it where you believe it is hidden. Unfortunately, it will eventually resurface in an inappropriate circumstance. If you respond to the body message, you can accept it and discover how to clear this debilitating vibration from your body and be free of it.

Hate often indicates fear. If you pay attention you will discover something you are afraid of and need to face. Since this could mean something from your past, it does require a spiritual perspective. The situation no longer exists, so you need to let it go to heal yourself. If you do not, you will make your body ill with the blocked emotions and past pains.

When you allow a world view that emotions are a communication from your body, you can be in charge of your life. You can respond appropriately in the present and heal yourself. If you respond to your body's emotional message, you learn what you are creating in your physical reality. You need to learn to let go of resistance to your emotions and listen to what is happening in your world so you can be in charge and create what you want.

Your judgemental views also block the more pleasant emotional messages. If you judge hate and do not acknowledge its presence in order to cleanse it, you will not have your attention for the creation of joy. Whenever you feel unhappy or caught in an emotional dilemma, you are not accepting something about yourself. When this aspect of self is faced, the "beast" is seen as your own creation and thus something with which you can deal. When you face and accept yourself as you are, without judgement, your healing begins.

We use emotions to keep in touch with what we are creating in the physical world. The body communicates the status of events to us with its emotions and it is our responsibility, as spirit, to respond to the message. We often create concepts, judgement and expectations that block us from owning and using the body's communication. We do this to avoid responsibility for our body and what we create through it.

Expectations are another block to clearing and allowing communication with the body for healing. When we expect ourselves to be perfect, we do not see ourselves as we are. Eventually we grow to dislike ourselves as we do not fulfill our expectations. We put these expectations onto ourselves and others and the expectations are always a lie. The lies then distort our perspective of reality and we become confused and unhappy. Every being with a body has lessons to learn and not all of them are pleasant. Thus we need to let go of our expectations in order to regain our spiritual perspective and accept ourselves as we are.

We have created and accepted ideas that the body is something evil to be overcome, rather than seeing it as our system for creativity and communication. We have invented entire ethical systems dictating how to relate to the body. We have then operated off of the beliefs that the body is to be avoided, beaten into submission or otherwise punished for its very existence. We have created the physical units, called bodies, to learn through, and then have set about avoiding the use and responsibility for them.

Thus our bodies have gained an inordinate amount of power in the physical realm, as we the spiritual beings have ignored or misused them. The more we have misused our bodies the less we have been able to use them for our spiritual purpose. The more seniority the bodies have gained, the less useful they have been to the beings. The more we created through the body's desires the less we created our spiritual purpose through the body.

Therefore, there is a need to re-establish the natural communication with the body. We need to do this to regain conscious spiritual control of the body and to create healing. We cannot create consciously and responsibly without knowing what is happening. Our healing process is dependent on our awareness of what we are creating in our body.

Other people's concepts can interfere with your awareness. When you use another person's ideas to create your world view, you block the effective use of your body. You adopt adults' ideas when you are a child and need to release any of those concepts that are no longer appropriate for you. You may have accepted a concept from your father that it is difficult to provide for your family. That may have been true for him during the Depression but it is not true for you now. If you do not let go of his way of seeing this, you will make providing for your family difficult when it does not need to be. If your mother believed that as a woman she could not receive, but always had to give to and nurture others, and you adopted this view, you will color your life with this concept. You could create a disease or some other physical problem from operating through another's concept.

If you have accepted someone else's way of operating in this world, this will distract you from your own strengths and abilities. A parent may have taught you to take responsibility for others so you would look after your younger sibling. This may have taken shape in your adult life as taking care of everyone except yourself. You have to let go of this old concept to be free to heal yourself and others. This idea could have been programmed into your system with pain, which would now manifest as fear if you do not take responsibility for others. The fear would really be fear of the pain of punishment, but would seem to be fear of not being responsible for others.

As children we accept and create many powerful concepts that are inappropriate and even damaging to us as adults. To heal ourselves we have to discover what these are and let them go. A foreign or inappropriate concept can cause damage to the physical and spiritual systems. Often a physical illness is a manifestation of a past pain experience or the attempt to operate through inappropriate concepts or energy, such as jealousy or hate. These and other creations such as pain, fear, loneliness, doubt and many others can cause physical illness. Letting go of these past pains is one way we heal. Forgiveness is a form of letting go. We are the ones who either created or accepted the inappropriate information, so we can as easily let it go. It is a waste of creative energy to blame someone else for our life experience and creative choices.

Key To Spiritual Balance

Many people believe that it is necessary to suffer or experience pain to evolve spiritually. This one concept can cause one to create a great deal of unnecessary misery. Unfortunately, many religions and societies adhere to this belief, so we are teaching it to our children. We can let go of this lie about how to live here on Earth and remember that we can create health and well-being more easily than we can create pain and suffering. Creating pain and suffering can be a misuse of the body. The difficulties and challenges in the spiritual journey are abundant enough without our having to pursue them.

Since you have been operating with your beliefs for so long, you believe they are yours even when you have adopted them from someone else. For example, during your birth, you may have picked up a belief from your mother that life is painful. You have had the belief all your life, so it would appear to you to be yours. It is necessary for you to learn what your vibration is so you can clear away anything that is not yours.

Concepts, ideas and words are all energy. When we change a concept or idea, we create healing. Old concepts from this life or a past life, or a concept that we accepted from someone else, can block us from achieving new goals. For example, if we believe that healing is done to us by someone else, then we block our ability to heal self. It is necessary to remove the old idea in order for the concept of self healing to flourish. Often we become resistant to past experiences, particularly if they were painful. This resistance forms a holding pattern with the past and we continue to create the same experiences. Healing requires that we let go of the past and foreign concepts so we can operate from our new beliefs in the present.

We have many ideas and concepts tied up in any significant word such as healing. Sometimes we have inappropriate information associated with a word. We could believe that someone else has to heal us, or that healing relates only to the body. If we believe that healing relates only to the body, then we seek a physical solution to any illness or physical difficulty. The answer may be there, but it may not. The answer to the problem may be found only from a spiritual perspective. Either way, the spiritual perspective provides peace and clarity. There are many illnesses that cannot be diagnosed or explained physically. Thus when we use the word healing we need to be aware of the spiritual as well as the physical significance. We need to cure the cause as well as the problem so we do not have to repeat the experience.

With a neutral spiritual perspective you can determine what you need to change and what is appropriate for you. This self-knowledge is gained through meditation. You develop a neutral view as you turn within and get to know yourself and your creations. This helps you see what to change and what to enhance. Self-knowledge is a necessary ingredient of healing. The spiritual perspective is needed to create healing on all levels.

The strictly physical perspective of healing is full of rules that are difficult, if not impossible, to follow. The body becomes the only focus, without consideration for the spiritual reality. With this focus, healing loses its joy and becomes serious, frightening and often impossible. We need to have our spiritual perspective and our awareness of how to harmonize with the body. All disease can be an opportunity to learn a spiritual lesson. If we do not recognize this, we keep repeating the mistakes until we learn.

An important part of healing is the balance between spirit and body. We are spirit manifesting through a physical body. We must learn how to operate as spirit in the physical world. We also have to teach the body to trust and accept us, and allow us to raise its vibration. This takes patience. We need to allow the body to operate as it does, with effort and through time and space. We also need to allow ourselves to be the immortal beings we are. This takes awareness of the differences between spirit and body and the acceptance of each as it is.

To heal we must see that we are each a spark of God. As a part of the Divine Force we can change anything in our system. If we have created hate or doubt in our body and it makes the body sick, we must see this and remove the cause as well as the illness. We need to see and accept ourselves as we are and forgive our own mistakes. If we have allowed our body to become dark, we can heal it by filling it with light.

We are immortal, knowing, powerful beings who are loved by God. We make mistakes as we learn and grow and must heal these, as a child heals a scratch made when falling down as he learns to walk. We are spirit; we are not our problems or other creations. When we see ourselves as spirit we can forgive ourselves for our mistakes and heal ourselves.

Everything is energy in motion. We can manipulate energy to create what we want. We need to allow our spiritual awareness of all forms of energy. We tend to become fixated on the visual physical perspective and forget the spiritual view. We need this spiritual perspective to create healing. When we see all things in motion we can consciously move the energy and create the change we want. We can bring light into the dark areas to cleanse and heal. This spiritual awareness is the avenue through which miracles flow.

We need to remember that our only required contracts are with our body and with God. When we are in harmony with ourselves as spirit, with our body and with God, our life experience flows. When we are not in harmony with either our body or our God, then we need to make a change or heal ourselves to get back in touch. The body aspect which we have touched on is important; however, the most important of all things is our relationship with our God.

As spirit there are many levels of awareness. There is the level of awareness we manifest in the body and there are many other levels of spiritual awareness that form the network or connection with God, Who is in and around us. This spiritual ethos is the path through which all life flows. All healing comes from God to our spiritual awareness level in the body. The more we open our awareness to our God, the more open we are to healing. As we bring in the light of God we bring in the light of healing.

God is in constant motion, is always changing and thus is healing. When we tune into this force of light and life, we begin to move and change without conflict. Healing can become a way of life when we focus on the Divine Source. Our habit is to focus on the body and to forget to focus on our Source of healing. When we see that we must turn inward to God to heal any aspect of self, whether it is of the body or of spirit, we find all things are possible.

In order to create healing, we need to turn within and quiet the busy demands of the body and the illusions of the physical world, to find our path to God. Meditation is the key to turning within and the beginning of self healing. Once the path to God within is established, one can turn inward for the information, strength and guidance for any healing need.

While there is a great deal of healing help available in this world, the ultimate decision for anything in our lives must come from us. Often fear blocks us from this awareness: our fear of our own power, of our total responsibility for our reality, or our fear of making a mistake. Fear can actually freeze us in our process and keep the healing from happening.

Often our fear comes from doubt: the doubt of our spiritual reality or the doubt caused by our seeming separation from our God. We have to re-establish our belief in ourselves as spirit and our belief in our Creator. This belief or faith is the foundation of all healing. As Jesus Christ always said, "Your faith healed you". He never claimed to heal the person. He always credited the individual's faith. This faith in self and God is essential for change to take place. Clear doubt from your thoughts and you heal yourself. Renew your faith in yourself as spirit and in your God and healing will occur.

HEALING

Since all healing flows from God it is necessary for us to set up our energetic system to receive the information from God. We may even need to restructure our body and the spiritual system associated with it to be able to receive the information and healing. This means turning within through meditation to discover what we have created in this physical reality and deciding what we need to change. Like any system, the one where we as spirit manifest into the physical body has correct working patterns and channels. Like the plumbing and electrical systems in our house, the body has a clear system for us to flow through. It is our responsibility to clear, unplug, rewire or do whatever we have to do to repair and maintain our system for communication with God.

Recognize yourself as a bright spirit expressing your creativity through a physical body and you will regain your joy in being here on Earth. Communicate with God and you will find whatever you need to create your experience in a healing manner. You have the God-given power to heal yourself. Have faith in yourself and God, and you will heal.

SELF HEALING TECHNIQUES

Since all healing is self healing we need to turn within to learn to know ourselves as spirit, our body and our relationship with God. There are techniques to help us do this. These techniques are simply ways of relating to our energy system to help cleanse and own it for our spiritual purpose. The techniques help us balance when we get out of balance. They can be used to assist us to create change in our reality in order to heal ourselves.

The techniques are like the ones used by a painter. There are many different painting techniques and each painter needs to discover the ones that work for him. We paint our canvas of life using the techniques we find which work for us. As we paint our life we need to maintain both our spiritual and our physical awareness, since we are creating as spirit in the physical world. Our life is like a painting. As a painter has a vision and puts it on a canvas, so we as spirit have an idea and manifest it in the body. If we do not like a brush stroke we can change it, just as we can heal anything in our life creations.

These techniques are presented to help you re-awaken to your spiritual self without losing touch with your physical creations. They draw your attention back into yourself where you can find your own information and your path to God. Within, you can find all the information you need and want without filtering it through someone else's system of beliefs.

All of the techniques can assist you to heal yourself as they help you cleanse and clear your personal space. You can use the techniques to clear others' concepts from your reality and to help you to let go of your own inappropriate concepts. You can use them to help you let go of past pain and detrimental emotions or behavior. The techniques help you heal yourself.

We are spirit and everything we do is a spiritual creation: our work, our relationships, everything. As we practice the techniques, we become conscious of ourselves as spirit creating through a body. As spirit, we are taking charge and not allowing the body or someone else's beliefs to run our lives. It can be exciting to experience this creative healing power.

These techniques can help you focus on yourself and your healing process. As you heal yourself, you become a healing force in the lives of everyone you know. As you heal, you change things in and around you. When you heal yourself, you heal others at the same time, as we are all one. The Golden Rule, "do unto others as you would have them do unto you", has greater meaning than most people realize. Since you are one with all things, you actually do unto yourself whatever you do unto others and vice versa. Be kind to everyone, including yourself, and you are healing our world.

To best experience these techniques, find a quiet place where you can be alone and undisturbed. Sit in a straight-backed chair with your spine as straight as possible. This helps your energy move more smoothly. Sit with your hands separated in your lap and your feet flat on the floor. Take a few deep breaths to relax your body and let yourself enjoy using the techniques to heal yourself.

AMUSEMENT

Amusement is essential to healing. Amusement is like the helium in our balloon: it keeps our energy up. When we are amused, we are light and everything flows smoothly and easily. When we are caught in the heavier energies of the body, such as anger, fear or hate, we find it difficult to move with such a heavy load.

Laughter changes the chemical balance of the body. Amusement brightens and lightens our spiritual and physical energies and brings balance back to our world. The comedians of our world are healers, as they help us laugh at ourselves and take life more lightly. They are the catalysts that bring amusement into our awareness. The amusement helps us heal ourselves. Amusement is similar to forgiveness. When we are amused, we can easily let go.

There are many stories about people who have used amusement to heal themselves. Some used it to heal a physical illness and some to heal emotional pain. Amusement can be used to heal anything in your life. You only need to discover it within yourself and let it bubble out and into your reality.

There is the story of the man who was sick and believed that God would heal him. One day his wife made him go to a doctor and the doctor told him that he could be healed with surgery. The man refused and said that God was going to heal him. Then his son brought a spiritual healer to the house and the healer told the man that he could heal himself by forgiving his father. The man said he didn't need to do that because God was going to heal him.

Then one day an angel appeared to the man and told him he would be healed if he would forgive himself. The man said he didn't need to do that because God was going to heal him. Well, the man died soon after that and went to heaven. There he met Saint Peter and complained about how God had not healed him. Saint Peter asked him what he had wanted! After all, God had sent him two healers and an angel.

When we can laugh at our own human foibles, we heal. The man, like all of us, had judgement about ways of healing and was not open to anything except his perfect idea. He was very serious and was not taking responsibility for himself. He wanted an "outside force" to fix his problem. Amusement would have helped fill his balloon so he could lighten up and heal himself by finding God and his answers within. With amusement he would have easily forgiven his father and himself. With the barrier of non-forgiveness removed, he would have experienced himself as spirit and his God. Amusement helps us be lighter so we can experience Light.

Nothing in our world is worthy of worry. Something may need attention but worry will not accomplish anything. Being serious and heavy will cause the job to take longer. Amusement will make any burden light and easy to carry. With amusement we can bear our earthly burdens lightly and assist others to bring light into their lives.

Play with your amusement. Think of something you are being serious about. Now think of something amusing about this trouble. Notice if your attitude changes when you allow yourself to see the amusing aspect of your creation. If you will put a funny face on your problems, you will find them easy to solve. If this idea is not serious enough for you, you can try being amused about how serious you are.

When things seem dark, just shine the light of amusement on them and the darkness will melt away. Be like a child using a shiny mirror to reflect sunlight into dark corners. Use your amusement with all of the healing techniques and you will find them fun and effective. Fill your problems, pains and healing projects with the helium of amusement and they will float away.

GROUNDING

Grounding is a connection between your first chakra, which is near the base of your spine, and the center of the earth. Chakras are energy centers located throughout your body; the main ones are located along the spine. Your first chakra contains the information about how to relate to this reality.

Your grounding helps you to be aware of and centered in this physical world. It allows you to connect your spiritual self to your physical body and to the planet. Grounding gives you a sense of ease and safety.

Grounding helps you heal yourself by giving you a conscious connection with this reality. It helps you be more aware and in control of your physical creations. When you are grounded, the body is under your control as you are more present and focused on it. Grounding makes the body feel safe as you are there and in charge, much as a child feels safe when an adult is present to help.

Grounding also gives you a way to release unwanted energy and concepts. You can let anything you no longer want flow down your grounding cord to the center of the earth to be neutralized. This energy can be reused in another form. Since you are constantly changing, grounding acts as a release system for whatever you need to cleanse. Just as your skin is constantly falling away and rebuilding itself, so you are constantly changing your perception of reality. As you mature spiritually you gain a broader view of all things, just as you do as you mature physically. Grounding is a powerful healing tool as it offers stability and release, through all of your changes and growth.

Grounding is a spiritual tool you can use to let go of anything you no longer want. It can be used to assist you to forgive by letting go. You can release the unwanted energy or emotion down your grounding cord and free yourself of burdens and pains.

To experience grounding, relax in your chair with your feet flat on the floor and your hands and feet separated. Take a few deep breaths to help yourself relax. Be aware of the space near the base of your spine where your first chakra is located. The chakras are located near ductless glands, so the first chakra is near the gonads. Since these glands are located in slightly different places in male and female bodies, the first chakra is also. It is the only chakra that is different in the two bodies. Women, your first chakra is between your ovaries. Men, your first chakra is just above your gonads.

From your first chakra create a cord of energy and let it flow, like a laser beam, down through the physical world of chair, floor and earth, to the center of the earth. Make the connection between your first chakra and the grounding cord a strong one. Also make a strong connection at the center of the earth. Breathe and relax your body, allowing it to adjust to being grounded.

You can be grounded at all times. It is an excellent technique to maintain constant control of your physical creativity. You can be grounded when you are sitting, standing, lying down, walking, or whatever. The more you practice your grounding, the more grounded you will be.

Practice your grounding now by standing up and walking around the room while you are grounded. Then sit back down and experience your grounding from this position. Close your eyes and experience being grounded for a few silent moments. Notice how this technique affects you and your body.

You create a healing for yourself whenever you ground, as grounding changes your relationship with your body and your creations by putting you in control. When you are grounded you can be in charge of your physical creativity. When you are in control as spirit you create from your spiritual perspective rather than from the body's desires.

Again be aware of your first chakra and create the grounding cord from your first chakra to the center of the earth. Be aware of your grounding. Breathe deeply and enjoy being grounded.

Notice if your body feels safer or more relaxed when you ground. If it does, it is welcoming you the being; if it does not, you need to clear a block to your body's acceptance of you. Ground and be aware of what your body is concerned about when you take control. Release the block down your grounding cord. Take a few deep breaths and relax with your grounding. You can repeat this as many times as you need, as you may have several concepts that block your body from feeling comfortable with grounding.

Let your grounding cord and your breathing relax your body. Open your communication with your body by grounding through it.

Be grounded and be aware of a belief that you have which blocks your self healing process. Accept whatever comes to your awareness. Let the belief go down your grounding cord to the center of the earth and be neutralized there. You can release this same belief several times, as you tend to hold beliefs in many ways and in several areas of your system.

Some of the confusion about healing comes from the mistaken idea that if you clear something once, you are finished with it. Actually, you may need to clear it from several levels of your system. If you believed the idea was valuable, you stored it in many places. Each time you release a block or disruptive belief you become more aware and can perceive that you need to continue to clear this idea until it is gone.

Any concept may be a powerful one for you or one that will take some time to clear from your system. Use your own inner knowing to determine the progress of your healing process.

Put your attention on your grounding cord. Notice if it is as energetic and strong as before. If you need to, strengthen it by adding more energy to the flow from your first chakra to the center of the earth. Sit quietly and relax with your grounding. Your grounding can be used to help you focus and become more spiritually aware by simply being. Ground and experience this quiet spiritual space now.

Grounding can be a foundation for your healing process.

THE CENTER OF YOUR HEAD

The center of your head is the place in your body where you can experience neutrality. It is the place where you can center in the body and be in charge of your creations. When you are in this neutral place, you have the ability to not judge yourself and others. Neutrality is a prerequisite to healing.

When you are in the center of your head you can see what is, rather than what you wish to see. It is possible to heal when you take this neutral view, as you can see clearly and are not working in the dark. The center of your head is the place in your body where you are least affected by your emotions or other people's emotions and ideas. When you are in neutral, you can stay above self-sympathy and other victim games which block healing. The center of your head gives you the spiritual view needed for healing.

Relax in your chair with your feet flat on the floor and your hands and feet separated. Take a few deep breaths and let yourself be present in the moment. Be sure your grounding cord is connected to your first chakra and to the center of the earth. Focus your attention into the center of your head, behind your eyes and up a fraction.

You are spirit and your body is your creative expression. When you as spirit enter your body, your body may react to your presence. This is when grounding is invaluable to help the body adjust to you, the more energetic being. Notice your grounding while you are in the center of your head. Allow this flow of energy from your first chakra to the center of the earth to help you release any tension caused by you being in the center of your head.

Breathe deeply and relax as you experience being grounded and in the center of your head. Allow the busyness of your thoughts to flow down your grounding cord. Sit quietly with your attention in the center of your head and be aware of yourself as spirit.

You may experience the bright light of energy which is you. This can help you realize that you are not just a body, you are spirit. If you do not see this bright light, be reassured that you are a bright being and that it may take some time for you to see yourself in the center of your head. Quietly continue to focus your attention into the center of your head in order to have this spiritual awareness. This awakening to yourself as spirit is a joyous healing experience. The awareness that you are spirit makes your healing easy and light.

HEALING

The center of your head is your neutral space where you can be in control of your reality. In order to learn to recognize that you are there, focus in other places and experience the difference. Move your awareness a foot above your head and then move back into the center of your head. Move to other places such as into your index finger or left big toe, and then back into the center of your head after each trip. By moving your attention to different places and back to the center of your head, you will more clearly identify when you are centered in your head.

Experience being in the center of your head. Be aware of something about yourself you wish to change. Be grounded and allow that which you wish to release to flow down your grounding cord and leave your body. Be aware of the neutral perspective from the center of your head. If you judge the aspect of you that you are healing, you will not let it go. The judgement will hold it. Practice focusing in the center of your head. Any time you experience judgement, move back to the center of your head. Release the judgement down your grounding, and then release the unwanted energy.

You are an immortal being and have created your body to learn and grow through here on Earth. The center of your head is the space from which you can perceive what is actually happening in your world, so you can determine how you wish to respond, if at all. Being in the center of your head is important in healing as you need to be able to see what is going on in order to know what you want to change. The center of your head also allows you a neutral, non-judgemental view where you are not overwhelmed by the body's needs, wants and emotions. The center of your head gives you the needed spiritual perspective for healing to take place.

When you focus in the center of your head and learn to see the world from there, you develop a new view of this reality. You find the spiritual becoming more important, the physical becoming less important. You realize that you are not a body but are spirit. The body's desires become less important. Healing naturally occurs as you enhance this spiritual perspective.

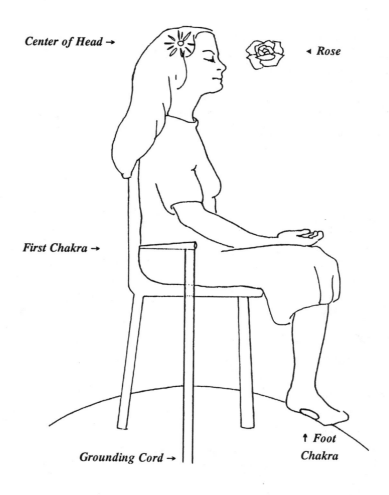

Figure 1. Center of Head & Creating and Destroying
a Rose

CREATING AND DESTROYING

Healing involves both creation and destruction. Everything is in constant motion. Motion is change and change involves all aspects of creative energy. Change requires both the creative and the destructive process, as when one thing ends another begins. The planet shows us this principle and our bodies display it also.

The planet heals itself with its seasons which have active and dormant periods for life processes. It heals itself with natural changes such as volcanos, earthquakes, fires and so forth, as it changes the environment to enhance new growth. Our bodies are constantly healing themselves as exemplified in the growth and loss of skin and hair. The body ingests and eliminates food, grows from a baby to an adult form, and creates new cells all during life. As the new form is created, the old form is destroyed.

Since healing is change, we have to include the full circle of creation and destruction to allow for healing. Unfortunately we have come to see destruction as "bad", when in reality it is an integral part of our creativity. We need to let go of our judgement to be able to see that our ability to destroy is part of our creativity on earth.

One main reason we have learned to judge destruction is that the death of the body has come to be something that is feared. The body's death is actually a natural part of our healing process. As spirit, we are immortal and create life experiences in many bodies. When we are through with the learning cycle in one body, we leave it to continue our learning process elsewhere. Death, or the destruction of our physical body, is part of the Divine plan to allow for our spiritual growth. When we leave one body, we are free to create a new one to learn our next lessons; just as we leave one grade in school and move on to the next. We need to finish the lessons designated for each body before moving to the next, just as we have to learn the lessons in first grade before we are allowed into the second grade. If we try to skip a lesson, we will have to repeat it until it is learned.

All of life is change, including birth and death. When we stop the change, we stop the healing. We can take conscious charge of our healing process by choosing what we wish to change. We can heal ourselves by becoming spiritually aware creators of our reality.

As spirit you create your experiences from your beliefs, so it is necessary to evaluate your beliefs to heal yourself. When you get to know the beliefs through which you create, you can understand your reality better. For example, if you believe that you are just a body, then you will be afraid of death. When you destroy that belief and see that you are an immortal spirit, you will begin to lose your fear of death. You will realize that death is only a phenomenon of the body and not of the spirit. If you believe that you have to suffer to grow, then you will create a great deal of unnecessary suffering in your life. Your belief in suffering as an ingredient of growth will cause you to create through suffering. By destroying this belief you can create a new belief that you can grow through joy. When you are not happy with your life, it is necessary to find the belief that is limiting your spiritual creativity and destroy it. When you destroy the limiting beliefs, you are able to create new beliefs which provide spiritual freedom.

The symbol of a rose is used in this technique. The rose is a symbol for the emergence of the soul in its awareness of God. As a rose turns to the sun for its light and life, so we are meant to turn to God as our source of light and life.

Be in the center of your head, ground yourself from your first chakra to the center of the earth. Create a mental image picture of a rose about six inches in front of your forehead. Admire the rose. Take a deep breath and relax as you enjoy your creativity.

Next, explode the rose. Simply let it disappear.

You have just exercised your God-given right to create and destroy in your own space. Your space is defined by your body and its energy system.

Create another rose and destroy or explode it. Practice creating and destroying the image of a rose until you feel comfortable with the technique. This process helps you clear your space as you are changing your energy.

You may find this helpful any time you are healing yourself. In fact you may need to create and destroy roses to help you ground and be in the center of your head.

Use this technique for specific healing projects.

Ground, be in the center of your head and create a rose. Be aware of something you wish to clear from your belief system. Let the belief go out into the rose and then explode the rose. For example, find a belief that blocks you from healing yourself. Put it into a rose and explode the rose. Do this several times until the belief is cleared from this level of your energy system.

Create a rose and explode it. Create a rose and release into it anything that prevents you from being aware that you are the creator of your reality and explode the rose. Continue to create and destroy roses until the concept that blocks you is cleared. Create another rose and explode it to clear any other energy which emerged during the cleansing process.

You can clear most concepts or energies from your space by putting them into a rose and exploding the rose. The more you practice, the more aware you will become, as you will be clearing your system during the process. You can use this technique to heal yourself by changing your view of life. You can clear doubt, hate, fear, pain or whatever you have blocking your healing energy. When you clear the debilitating beliefs, you are free to create with your spiritual clarity.

When you destroy the beliefs that limit you to a physical perspective and create beliefs that enhance your spiritual perspective, you regain your joy in creating your reality. Your belief in God and your belief in yourself help you find the path through the physical maze. By changing your beliefs and allowing a spiritual perspective, you heal yourself.

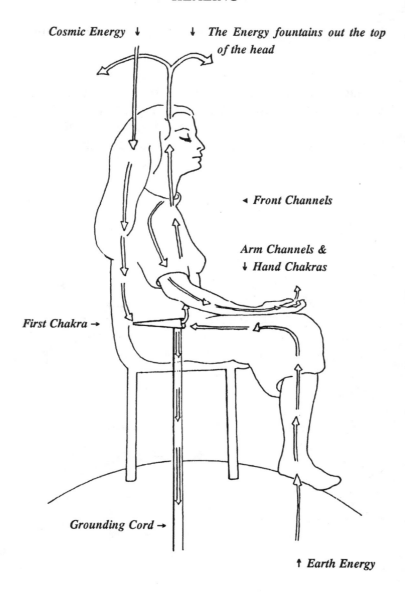

Figure 2. Running Energy

RUNNING ENERGY

Everything is energy and all energy is in motion. Systems do not function properly when an energy flow is disrupted. We need to learn how to discover any block to our flow of energy and how to clear that block. The technique of running energy is a way of consciously moving our energies through our system to enhance the flow and act as a constant cleanser. Consciously running energy is a healing process.

We are already spirit and do not need to become more spiritual. We simply need to be more aware of ourselves as spirit. We do not need to be separate from the earth or worldly things to be spiritual; we simply need to be senior to the physical world and remember that we are spirit and in charge of our earthly creations. Running energy helps us remember how to balance our spiritual awareness with our earthly creativity. Consciously running energy is a spiritual healing process. We can do it daily. Just as we bathe our body, we can spiritually cleanse ourselves by running our energies to clear our system.

EARTH ENERGY

Earth energy is the energy of our planet. Since we are using schoolhouse Earth to learn our spiritual lessons, we need to know how things work here. The conscious use of earth energy helps us identify with and use our planet to learn our spiritual lessons.

Part of the lesson in any lifetime is how to operate a body and how to function in time and space. The body and the planet are ours through which to create and learn. We have to own this physical reality and attach to it in order to operate fully in it. It is necessary to heal our bodies and get in harmony with our earthly creations in order to accomplish our spiritual purpose here.

Create your grounding cord from your first chakra to the center of the earth. Focus your attention behind your eyes in the center of your head. From this neutral place be aware of the bottoms of your feet. You have chakras in the arches of your feet. These chakras, or energy centers, can be opened and closed like the lens of a camera. Open your feet chakras. Bring earth energy up through these chakras and through the channels in your legs to the first chakra, near the base of your spine. Allow the excess earth energy to flow down your grounding cord.

Be grounded and centered and relax with this flow of earth energy up through your feet chakras and leg channels, to your first chakra and down your grounding cord. Breathe deeply and allow the energy to run. Let the earth energy act as a cleansing flow, washing away any blocks in your feet chakras or leg channels. Allow time to enjoy this healing process and the flow of healing energy from the earth.

You can run earth energy any time and place. Use it to heal your body and your relationship with the planet.

COSMIC ENERGY

Cosmic energy is the unlimited energy from the Cosmos. This is the infinite flow from the Cosmic Consciousness. Cosmic energy is vibrations of energy or light. We often see these vibrations in the form of color. All spectrums of energy or color are available.

Cosmic energies can be used to create within our physical world. Cosmic energy is essential in healing. We use these energies to change our vibrations and to balance our energy systems. Colors can be described in terms of hot and cold. Cosmic energy can also be viewed this way. When our energy system is running hot, we can use a vibration to cool it, or vice versa. All things require a certain balance to maintain life. Our use of cosmic energies assists us to balance our reality and heal ourselves. We know that the body has a certain tolerance to hot and cold. We also need to be aware that we as spirit require balance. We have to learn to adjust our energy in relation to all dichotomies to heal ourselves. Either extreme can be unhealthy for spirit or body.

Cosmic energies are like the tools in a carpenter's workshop. There is every possible vibration available for any circumstance or need, just as there is a tool available for every job. We need to be open to all the varieties of energy available in order to have our full healing potential. We do not need to limit our use of a vibration because we judge it. All vibrations have their purpose.

We will use a gold vibration for self healing as it is a neutral energy. We will also use a blue energy to allow you the experience of another vibration. Light blue is often associated with healing, although it is not exclusive in its healing power.

Ground from your first chakra to the center of the earth. Focus your attention behind your eyes in the center of your head. Bring earth energy up through your feet chakras, through the channels in your legs to the first chakra and allow the excess energy to flow down your grounding cord.

Refocus your attention into the center of your head. Above your head create a gold sun and allow the energy to flow down to the back of the chakra at the top of your head. This is your seventh chakra, which contains your ability to know. Allow the energy to continue to flow down your back through channels on each side of your spine.

When the gold energy reaches your first chakra allow it to mix with the earth energy. Bring the mixture of cosmic and earth energies up the channels running up through your body. These channels are on either side of your chakras.

When the energy reaches the top of
your head, let it fountain out and flow all
around you. Be in the center of your head and
experience the flow of energy as it moves
through you, cleansing your system.

From the center of your head focus on
the cleft of your throat and allow some of the
energy to move from there through channels in
your shoulders, down your arms and out the
palms of your hands. Be focused in the center
of your head, check your grounding and enjoy
the flow of energies.

Running your earth and cosmic energies is a way
of cleansing your spiritual energy system. The flow
acts like water, washing away impurities, blocks and
so forth. You are cleansing blocks to your flow of
energies. You are washing away foreign and
debilitating energies. This process of running energy is
a method of healing yourself without effort. Since you
have a wealth of vibrations to use in this healing
process, it helps to practice using these consciously.
You can use any vibration you like. You have used the
neutral gold energy and now can try the blue healing
energy.

Be in the center of your head and
grounded. Be aware of how the gold vibration
affects your body. Then release the gold
energy down your grounding cord. Now create
a ball of light blue energy above your head and
let that flow down through the top of your head
to the channels along each side of your spine
all the way to the first chakra. Mix the blue
cosmic energy with earth energy and allow it to

flow up through the body and out the top of your head. Allow the energy to flow through the channels in your shoulders and arms to your hands, and let the energy flow out your hands.

Run this blue vibration of energy for a few minutes. Be aware of how your body reacts to it. Be aware of how you like to use this vibration. Notice any differences between the blue and the gold energy.

After using the blue energy for a few moments, let it flow down your grounding cord and out of your system. Create a ball of the gold vibration above your head and let the gold energy flow down your back channels to your first chakra. Mix your earth and cosmic energies and let them flow up your front channels and fountain out the top of your head. Allow energy to flow down your arm channels and out your hands.

When you decide to stop consciously running your energies, bend forward and dangle your hands toward the floor. Bending forward releases energy from your head, shoulders, arms and hands. When you are ready, sit up and continue your healing exercise or return to your daily schedule.

Allow a period of time every day to heal yourself by running your energy. It may take time for you to experience the results of this technique, or you may be aware of changes in yourself immediately. Everyone is unique; thus your experience of these techniques will be unique.

HEALING

When you make grounding, being in the center of your head and running energy part of your day, you make self healing part of your life. If you have considerations about the time this will take, ask yourself if you would forgo your bath because you did not have time. Healing yourself needs to be at the top of your list of necessary activities every day.

Most people find they can be quiet for fifteen to twenty minutes to begin with and eventually increase their practice to thirty minutes to an hour. You can divide these sessions into shorter segments until you train your body to be still. The important thing is to run your energies daily and make grounding a constant. This way you are allowing your energies to flow and you are living your healing process.

When you have a specific healing project, you can run your earth and cosmic energies to cleanse and heal yourself by focusing on the specific issue. By grounding, centering, using the flow of earth and cosmic energies and your ability to create and destroy a rose for the specific focus, you clear your spiritual space. This spiritual clarity and your amusement will create a healing environment for you.

While there is a great deal of healing help available in this world, the ultimate decision for anything in our lives must come from us.

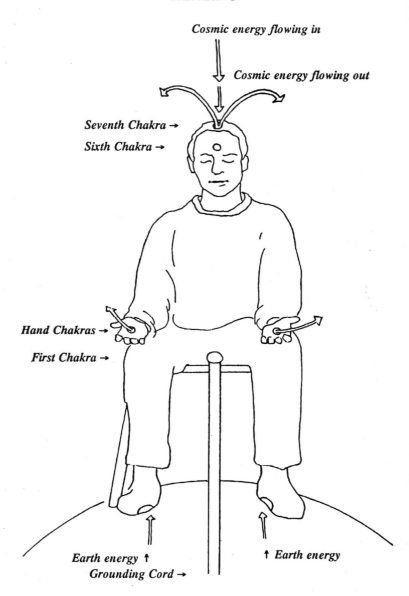

Figure 3. Chakras: Healing Centers

CHAKRAS: HEALING CENTERS

There are four main areas where healing energy is concentrated in the spiritual system. Healing can relate to any of the chakras, but these chakras are necessary for healing. They are: the first chakra, located near the base of the spine; the sixth chakra, located in the center of the head; the seventh chakra, located on the top of the head; and the hand chakras, located in the palms of the hands.

The first chakra has our information about how to relate to this physical reality. The sixth chakra has information on how to see clearly as spirit. The seventh chakra relates to our ability to know spiritually and to communicate with the spiritual realm. We use the hand chakras when we heal and create in the physical world.

We need the information in each of these energy centers in order to gain the perspective we require for healing. We have to know how to operate in this reality, how to see clearly what is happening, know how to deal with it and be able to manifest the change. This may seem like a lot to be aware of at once, but the healing flow is something that occurs automatically when we are tuned in to the spiritual and grounded in the physical.

Create your grounding cord from your first chakra to the center of the earth. As you do this, be aware of your first chakra near the base of your spine. Be aware of your information about how to relate to planet Earth and to your body. Use your grounding to help you take conscious control of your first chakra. Be aware of anything you wish to release that interferes with your control of your life and release it down your grounding cord.

Be aware of anything in your first chakra that blocks your healing energy and release it down your grounding cord.

Bring your first chakra to its highest healing vibration and use your grounding cord to release anything which interferes with this level of your healing energy. Simply believe it, and it will happen.

Focus your attention in the center of your head. Be aware of your ability to see clearly as spirit. Create a rose and release any block to your clear seeing into your rose and destroy the rose. For example, you may want to release any fear you have about being different. Be aware of anything in your sixth chakra that interferes with your healing energy and release it down your grounding cord.

Be in the center of your head and bring your sixth chakra to its highest healing vibration. As you do this, release any block to this vibration down your grounding cord. Allow yourself to increase your healing energy.

Now be aware of your seventh chakra on the top of your head. Be aware of your spiritual information and communication and own this chakra for yourself. It is not appropriate for any other being to have its energy in any of your chakras and particularly not in your seventh chakra. To release any foreign energy from this chakra, create a rose in front of you and let the foreign energy go into the rose and explode the rose.

Bring the seventh chakra to your highest healing vibration. Be still and know yourself as spirit and your ability to heal yourself. Use your grounding cord to release any interference to this knowing and healing. Create a rose in front of you and release into it any concept that blocks your healing energy in your seventh chakra and explode the rose.

From the center of your head be aware of your hands. There are chakras in the palms of your hands. Bring your hand chakras to their highest healing vibration and use your grounding cord to release any interference to this healing energy. Notice your hands and feel the energy flowing from them. You can put one hand above the palm of the other and feel this flow of healing energy. Create roses and explode them to release any blocks to the flow of healing energy through your hands. Allow the flow of energy to cleanse any blocks.

Feel the energy flowing out of the palms of your hands. Notice if it is warm or tingly or both. Healing energy often feels this way. Your hands may become warm and moist when you run a great deal of healing energy. Take one hand and move it above the other arm and hand, feeling the energy flow from the cleft of your throat down your arm and out your hand. Then switch hands and feel the energy flowing through the opposite arm and hand. You are feeling your own healing energy and learning to recognize it.

Again focus in the center of your head and enhance your grounding cord. Create and destroy roses to clear any blocks to the flow of your healing energy. Release energy down your grounding to enhance your healing process by cleansing any blocks to your healing energy flow. Be still and experience the flow of healing energy through your system. Enjoy this flow of cleansing energy.

These chakras contain a wealth of information. You need to be still and tune in to the healing energy within them to use them effectively. Simply bringing these chakras to your highest healing vibration each day can enhance your self healing. Combining this increase in healing energy with the techniques of grounding, centering, creating and exploding roses, increasing your amusement and running energy creates a powerful healing process. Be aware that all of this creates change, so allow time for your body to adjust to your healing changes.

Focusing in the center of your head helps you be neutral about your changes. If you experience doubt or confusion you can ground and center and use the other techniques to regain your spiritual perspective.

Gentleness and patience help you heal. As you are kind to yourself, you learn to be kind to others. Your internal gentleness will eventually flow out to the world.

PRESENT TIME

The concept of present time is so simple we often get out of touch with it. We try to intellectualize time and then get confused. We as spirit do not need to operate in time unless we are in a body. Together with God we have created time in order to focus our attention and help us learn our lessons. Time gives us an opportunity to correct mistakes.

In this physical reality time appears as a line with a past, present and future. As spirit, we have to learn to have our attention in the present, as this is where the body functions. In spiritual reality there is no time, but we have to relate to the physical reality when in a body and learn to deal with this illusion of time. We are learning about how to manipulate energy, so we sometimes put our attention in the past or future. We may be trying to solve a past problem or figure out a possible future. When we do get out of present time, our body gets confused or disturbed if we do not know what we are doing.

Present time is where we most easily create our physical reality. If we are not in the present, we are not in touch with our body. Present time is where we can be aware of what is happening and can respond to our creations.

Since there is no time for us as spirit, we can easily be drawn into past or future time and we need to bring our attention back to the present to accomplish our goals in this body. Grounding and running energy can help us clear our bodies so we enjoy being in present time.

If we are in the past, the body usually feels depressed or apathetic. If we are focused in the future, we often feel afraid as the body cannot be there yet. When we are in present time, the body is comfortable as this is the time in which the body operates. Simply putting our attention in the present can be a healing. Being in the present eliminates depression and fear caused by focusing our attention in the past or future.

Here and now, in the present, we have our power and our ability to heal. We cannot go to the past and change it; but we can change our view of the past and thus heal it. When we focus our attention in the present, our spiritual power and awareness are available for us to use. If we are projected into the past or future, we are not energetically available to ourselves or others. We can heal or change the past and future by acting now, in the present.

When we operate in the present and let go of the past, we can heal past pains and problems. As we run our energies, create and destroy roses and use our grounding, we release the past and allow ourselves to create what we want in the present. By focusing in the present, we focus our power, like the sun focused through a magnifying glass. We are present, so we can see what we need to release from past experiences in order not to repeat them in the future. When we are focused in present time, we can create what we want and not what we are resisting from the past or fantasizing about in the future.

At times we uncover something in our reality that we find difficult to deal with in the body. We can go out of the body to work through the problem and then bring the information back to our physical consciousness. When we work outside of the body we move out of the limits of time and can heal past and future experiences. One way we naturally go out of our body is at night when we sleep. While the body sleeps, we work as spirit outside of the physical body. We use the astral body, or energy body, to learn and heal through while we are out of the physical body. These out-of-body experiences can help us heal our physical body and solve our problems in this reality. The old saying "sleep on the problem" is a wise one as we can heal spiritually outside of the body and bring the effects of that healing back to our physical body. Many revelations and healing miracles have been brought back to physical awareness from out-of-body experiences.

When we combine consciously healing our physical body with awakening our awareness of our out-of-body experiences, we create a powerful healing flow. We can do this by running energy, grounding, centering and using the healing techniques daily.

God is in present time. God is spirit and spiritual reality does not have the illusion of past and future, therefore God is always in the present. To most easily fulfill our two agreements, with our body and with

God, we need to be in the present as much as possible. Our point of healing power is now.

To experience present time, create your grounding cord, focus into the center of your head, take a few deep breaths and relax your body. From the center of your head be aware of your body. Feel your heart beat. Experience your breathing. Feel your skin. Listen to your body's sounds. Use your awareness of your body to bring your attention into the present moment.

Check to be sure you are grounded and in the center of your head. Create a rose and release anything blocking you from being in the present into the rose and explode the rose. Repeat, releasing blocks to being in the present and exploding them in a rose as often as you like. We have all created many blocks to enjoying the present.

Ground, be in the center of your head. Run your earth energy up through your leg channels to your first chakra and down your grounding cord. Let the earth energy be in present time and melt away any energy that is not in the present.

Create a ball of gold energy above your head and let the energy flow down the channels on each side of your spine to the first chakra and mix with the earth energy. Bring the mixture of energies up through the channels in your body and allow it to fountain out the top of your head. Let some energy flow from the cleft of your throat out your arms and hands.

Bring the cosmic energy into present time and allow this present time energy to melt away anything in your system that is not in the present.

Focus your awareness in the present. Use your psychic techniques of grounding, centering and running energy and your awareness of your body's reality to bring your attention into the present. Experience the healing power of present time. Healing takes place in the present.

When you focus your attention into the present, you are focusing on your body and able to focus on your God, which are both always in the present. Since your required contracts for any lifetime are with God and with your body, when you are in the present you can fulfill these agreements and accomplish your spiritual goals. The present is where you have power, healing and your communication with God. Healing occurs in present time.

HEALING BRINGS GROWTH

As you heal yourself, you grow and change. You learn new ways to view reality and you need to remember to clear your old patterns or habits to make way for the new. You will become confused when you try to see the world through both the old and the new concepts at the same time. In time you will let go of your old beliefs and operate from the new ones as you practice your spiritual healing techniques.

When you heal yourself, you grow in your spiritual awareness. This growth can cause you to feel uncertain about yourself, as you are creating new perspectives and feel vulnerable with the unfamiliar ideas. You may need to reassure yourself that it is permissible to feel this way during your healing. You need to be willing to be as a child to enjoy this continuous learning process. Children are always learning and growing and we need to be as open to our growth to achieve our spiritual maturity.

Our spiritual growth is a continuing process. It never stops. You have always been creating new beliefs and destroying or clearing old ones. The times of uncertainty or vulnerability come when you are changing very rapidly. You may feel overwhelmed with the changes when you create major shifts in your perspective. For example, changing from believing that you are just a body, to seeing that you are an immortal spirit, will change your view of every aspect of your life.

You will be changing during the remainder of this life and throughout all of your incarnations in different bodies. As you learn how to manipulate your energy consciously through self healing and meditation, you begin to feel more competent and in control. Whenever you feel confused or upset, you can sit quietly and use the techniques to clear the old and make way for the new.

Ground, be in the center of your head and run your earth and cosmic energies. Create a rose, be aware of an old belief that is now blocking your healing process, put it into the rose and explode the rose. Be centered, grounded and run your earth and cosmic energies, using them to wash away old energies which block your present growth process. Relax and enjoy the quiet healing time.

Life is a process of growth. Give yourself permission to rejoice in your healing process by clearing the blocks to your growth. Be as a child, so you can enjoy learning and growing and healing. Play with your new techniques so they can assist you to cleanse anything in your way of enjoying your spiritual creativity.

When you enjoy your internal seasons, as you do those of our planet, you find yourself at peace with your growth. You become accepting of the fact that you are always growing and changing just as our planet is. With the healing comes new awareness of your spiritual self and the discovery of your internal power. Enjoy the fall, winter, spring and summer of your growth, and life will take on new meaning and brightness for you.

Growth is part of life and healing is growth.

HEALING

As a rose turns to the sun for its light and life, so we are meant to turn to God as our source of light and life.

GUIDED HEALING EXERCISE

Using the techniques and being aware of your chakras can assist you in your healing process. Grounding, being in the center of your head, creating and destroying roses, running earth and cosmic energies, being amused and being in present time are all techniques to assist you in your healing. They help you focus within and put your attention on your healing vibrations, as well as on the beliefs and blocks you need to change. The techniques help you focus in present time and acknowledge the healing power you have to change anything within you.

With the techniques to help you focus your healing energies, you simply need to be still and use them. As you use the techniques, you will discover the things on which you need to focus your healing energies. With you attention inwardly focused you will see what needs healing. You may begin with a body problem or you may need to put your attention on healing a spiritual imbalance. Either way, let your quiet time reveal to you where your healing attention is most needed in the present.

HEALING

You must use the techniques for them to work for you. Set aside a time each day for your self healing and the changes will come. As you focus your healing vibrations consciously, you will take charge of your creativity and your healing process. Determination is an important ingredient to help you stay with the daily healing focus.

GROUND. Create your grounding cord from your first chakra to the center of the earth. Connect the grounding cord firmly to your first chakra and to the center of the earth. Breathe deeply and release any energy down your grounding cord which would interfere with your self healing.

BE IN THE CENTER OF YOUR HEAD. Experience that bright light that is you in the center of your head. Take a deep breath and allow your body to experience the healing of your spiritual presence. Let the body relax with you; and allow yourself to accept your body.

BE AMUSED. From this grounded neutral space be amused about one of your healing projects. Be aware of an amusing aspect of it. Release seriousness down your grounding. Fill yourself with the light of amusement.

CREATE A ROSE. Release any block you have to healing yourself into the rose.

EXPLODE THE ROSE. Let the block to your self healing be destroyed with the rose.

CREATE AND EXPLODE ROSES. With each rose release any block to healing yourself into the rose and let go of the block as you explode the rose. Admire your healing energy as you do this. You are creating change in your energy system. You are healing yourself.

RUN YOUR EARTH ENERGY. Bring the healing vibration of the earth up through the chakras in your feet, through the channels in your legs to your first chakra. Let the energy flow down your grounding cord to the center of the earth. Experience the healing power of this energy as it clears and cleanses your system.

RUN YOUR COSMIC ENERGY. Create a ball of bright gold energy above your head. Let the energy flow down to the top of your head and down the channels on each side of your spine to the first chakra. Mix the earth and cosmic energies at the first chakra and bring the energy up through the body to fountain out the top of your head and flow around your body. Let some of the energy flow from the cleft of your throat down your arm channels and out the chakras in the palms of your hands.

RUN YOUR ENERGIES. Be grounded and in the center of your head and experience the healing flow of earth and cosmic energies through your system. Breathe deeply and enjoy the cleansing created by this flow of energies.

HEALING

Allow the energies to clear away any blocks to your self healing.

BE IN PRESENT TIME. Focus in the center of your head and be grounded in the present. Pull your attention into the present by listening to the body pulses. Let the flow of energies draw your attention to the present moment. Create and destroy a rose for anything blocking your attention from being in the present.

HEAL YOURSELF. Ground, center, allow the earth and cosmic energies to flow. Create and destroy roses for any interference to your self healing. Use the following suggestions or a focus of your own.

Create a rose and allow any body pain to go into the rose and explode the rose.

Create a rose and allow any emotional pain to go into the rose and explode the rose.

Create a rose for anything blocking your faith and explode the rose.

Use your grounding and flow of energies to wash away any unwanted energies.

Create a rose and allow any doubt to go into the rose and explode the rose.

Create a rose for anything blocking your healing process and explode the rose.

Release foreign or unwanted energies down your grounding cord.

INCREASE YOUR HEALING VIBRATION. Ground and be in the center of your head. Be aware of your first chakra and bring the healing energy to your highest vibration. Be aware of your sixth chakra and then your seventh chakra, bringing them both to your highest healing vibration. Also bring your hand chakras to their highest healing vibration.

ASK FOR HEALING GUIDANCE. Ground, center, run your energies and focus in present time. Bring the gold energy into the top of your head and let it flow through you. As all healing flows from God, be still and allow yourself to receive from God.

You can simply be still and receive, or you can ask specific questions, such as:

How can I best heal myself?

What spiritual lesson am I to learn from my healing process?

How can I heal my relationship with my body?

Please send me healing energy.

Create and destroy roses to clear any interference to receiving energy and information.

Sit quietly in the center of your head and you will receive the information you need. It is necessary for you to be still to hear it and allow yourself to have it.

HEALING

Be in the center of your head and experience your flow of healing energy. Relax the body and allow this healing.

When you are through with your healing exercise, bend forward and release energy from your head, shoulders and arms. Sit up and allow your energy to be at a comfortable vibration for you and your body to continue your daily activities.

Following these exercises daily will bring you spiritual awareness and a renewed healing energy. Persevere whenever you experience difficulties and the techniques will assist you to move through the problems. Have faith in the process and it will work for you.

HEALING OTHERS

While we can assist other souls in their healing process, we cannot do the healing for them. The person receiving healing attention must be in agreement with and allow the change, or it will not happen. The healer is a catalyst in the healing process. Both the healer and the healee must have faith in the process or the healing will not manifest.

The techniques are for self healing. When we are healed or clear, we can better assist others. The greatest healing we can offer another is the impact of our clear energy field. By bringing spiritual awareness into the physical reality, we heal ourselves and others.

An example of a healer is a midwife. While the mother and the baby are the creators of the birth experience, the midwife is the helper chosen by them to assist. She is there to encourage, direct, and assist when necessary. She does not give birth, nor is she born. The midwife healer is a catalyst and a helper. Ideally, she will help with both the physical needs and the spiritual opportunities, as birth is a time that the spiritual and physical realms are naturally open to one another. As healer, she is there to help, to guide and to encourage. The healer is the catalyst to change, the energy booster to raise the vibration for the highest possible healing level.

Healers, or those with the desire and energy to assist others, tend to forget that we cannot solve anyone else's problems. We can be a healing presence, a steadfast friend, an encourager, a catalyst and much more; we can lend a helping hand, but we cannot actually learn that person's lesson for her. We often try to take responsibility for another person's emotions as a way of trying to heal her. In reality, it only communicates that we do not believe she can solve her problem. We get involved in trying to solve the problem our way, and begin to create spiritually in the other soul's universe. The other person then has to clear our vibration from her system, as well as solve her original problem. We have to clear our ego involvement to be an effective healer.

We often communicate with one another with our emotions. We may then experience the other person's emotions as if they were our own. We need to release anyone else's emotions immediately after a communication as foreign emotions can feel overwhelming and can disrupt our own self-awareness. Holding another's emotions blocks our healing energy, as it disrupts our communication with self and our ability to respond to that other person.

If a friend is experiencing fear and you let that emotion overwhelm you, then you are two frightened people. If you allow the friend his own emotion and maintain yours, you are able to help your friend with your amusement or compassion or whatever you are experiencing.

This maintenance of personal space and focus on individual experience is essential in healing. We need to clear any foreign energy or concepts from our body and energy system, as others' concepts cause confusion. Each individual needs to be allowed his own experience to accomplish his goals. If we experience another's reality, we cannot learn our own lessons and he cannot learn his. If we do not allow ourselves to be separate and unique, we will see the world through both our own ideas and the other person's ideas at the same time. This is like a double negative photograph and is as confusing as one picture superimposed on another.

This practice of allowing each soul to solve its own problems is a difficult one as it takes a great deal of unlearning. We have all been taught to take care of others instead of ourselves. If each of us takes care of our own creations, we do not need to take care of each other's creations. Then we can be clear and free to respond to one another. This is not a popular view of reality, as it means that each soul has to take responsibility for self and all of its creations, even the ones we do not like.

In other words, when you clear yourself, you become a more effective helper or healer than when you try to heal or change everyone else. This gives each individual his own power. You need to clear and heal yourself before you can help others. Jesus stated it by saying "Do not judge the speck in your brother's eye, but first remove the log from your own eye." Heal yourself first. When you are healed, you will automatically affect others in a healing manner. As the flight attendants say every time you fly, "put your oxygen mask on first and then assist the child to put on his". If we are not breathing, then we are certainly not able to help anyone else.

We have learned to respond to others' problems in many ways that are not healing. One emotional response, which is actually invalidating to another person, is sympathy. We have forgotten that empathy allows us to understand and assist, while sympathy communicates a lack of faith in the other soul's ability to heal herself.

When we are in sympathy, we become like the person we are supposedly helping. For example, if a friend falls in a well and we go into sympathy, we jump down into the well with him. Then we have two people down a well. If we allow ourselves to experience empathy, which is a more neutral perspective, we can assist our friend. We can toss our friend a rope and pull him out of the well.

When we are assisting others to heal themselves, we cannot do it from sympathy. If we say, "Oh, you poor thing, what a terrible thing you have created", we make him feel helpless and weak. If we say, "You are a powerful being and you can change this, may I assist?", then we strengthen him by affirming our faith in him. Hopefully we can assist him to develop the necessary faith in himself for the healing to occur.

Empathy is similar to compassion. We can experience a sense of oneness with each other, without becoming the other. We actually need to maintain some distance to help that other person get back on firm ground. If we step into the quicksand with her, we are both sunk. If we stay on firm ground, we can help her get there too. With sympathy we become the other person and her problem and cannot assist, since we put ourselves where she is. When healing, we need to allow respect for the other person's creation. We need to notice if we are sympathetic and invalidating, rather than compassionate and helpful.

In healing much of our process is to open to God and become more spiritually aware. To heal self and become a more effective healer for others, we have to unlearn old habits and patterns that do not work. Sympathy is an old habit that does not work in healing. It is how we have been taught to respond, so we have to pay attention to our behavior to clear that pattern.

One way to avoid sympathy is to ask how you would feel if someone were sympathetic to you in the same circumstance. You may find yourself getting angry if you are the type of person who believes you can do what you need to do. Sympathy shows a lack of faith in God. How can we be sympathetic with a part of God? Each of us is a spark of the Divine Force. Who can honestly be in sympathy with such power?

You cannot give anyone anything you do not have yourself. In fact, you share what you have created. If you are creating love, faith, and healing in yourself, you will share these qualities. If you are filling yourself with pain, fear, doubt and hate you will share these vibrations. Therefore you must heal yourself in order to be a healing presence for others. Your own self healing process is your first priority, even when you are focused on assisting others. Personal responsibility and faith are keys to healing and we cannot give these to another soul. Each of us has to learn personal responsibility and develop faith for ourselves. We can teach these things to others only by living them ourselves.

The one place that you are in control is within your own space. You have the power within yourself to change anything you wish to change. The key is to turn within. As you clear yourself, you automatically assist others in the process. It is impossible to intellectualize the spiritual reality that we are all one, yet when you realize this, you realize that self healing is healing for everyone.

When one has the healing drive, whether it is focused inwardly or outwardly, one must learn self-control. Healers love to give, so there is the temptation to "overheal". Most healers enjoy giving so much that they cannot imagine anyone would not enjoy receiving all they have to give. All you have to do to understand this is to remember how you felt when someone kept giving to you when you did not want more. Whether someone is pushing more food on you or forcing you to hear more about yourself than you want to hear, it is an invasion of space. If you want to hear the information, receive the food or change your energy, it is not an invasion, as you are receptive and in agreement. If you do not want whatever is offered, the giver can be overhealing and invading your space by trying to force something on you.

Giving is not all "good" or beneficial. Giving and healing can be used in a detrimental manner. A healer can start believing he knows what is best for another and try to push his ideas onto the healee. This is not healing, but many try to believe that it is. It is important to eliminate the ego from healing. In fact when the ego is involved healing is blocked. Healing requires the agreement of all concerned. If you find that people sometimes seek distance from you when you believe that you are healing, you may be overhealing and they may be seeking their personal space. Overhealing gets you the opposite of what you seek.

If you overheal, a defense mechanism may come into play. If you overheal yourself, you may have a body reaction, such as having to sleep a great deal, or needing to eat a lot, or experiencing irritation. Overhealing can even cause the body to become ill as it does not have time to adjust to the changes you create as spirit. If you overheal another person, she may try to avoid you or be rude to you to push you away, as she tries to find her personal space and own healing pace.

We also need to be aware that there are those who do not want to be healed. Some people want to be where they are and do not have any desire to change. There are those who like what they have created, even when it is misery, and have come to embrace it as their way of life. We have to accept where everyone is and allow them their choice. We need to let go of those who do not wish to change and let them be as they are. This is a challenge for a healer, as healers want to change and improve and make well. We have to realize that there are times when the greatest healing is to do nothing and to allow the soul to find his own way "home". If we put our attention on a soul who does not wish to change, we can create damage to our own system. It is necessary to know when to let go.

HEALING

We can help others see themselves more clearly as we develop our own clarity. With our clarity we can see and accept each soul as it is. By consciously using the healing chakras, we can be our own self-healer and a healing presence for others. By clearing our own space and bringing in our own healing energy, we emerge as healers. By grounding, centering, running energy and tuning in to the information we have stored in the first, sixth, seventh and hand chakras, we develop our healing abilities and clarity. We need to constantly remind ourselves to bring our attention back to ourselves, as that is where the healing begins. Healing cannot flow from us unless it is within us. We cannot give anything we do not have. When we are healed and balanced, we provide this healing presence for others.

We all have a desire to heal ourselves and others, whether this desire is buried or conscious. An easy way to reawaken or increase this healing ability is to use it. By giving of ourselves, we heal ourselves and others. Whether we are talking, teaching, listening, doing something for someone, being amused or sharing our quiet healing presence, it does not matter. The important thing is the continuous giving of self. Giving from obligation is not the same thing. We have to give just as we have to breathe, because it is an essential spiritual quality. We are here to learn and grow and heal ourselves and the easiest way to do that is to interact with others in a healing manner. Giving is like all circles, it has two halves. The other part is receiving. When we give and receive in balance, our healing drive is satisfied and we are at peace.

SPIRITUAL BALANCE

The word miracle is from the Latin word *mirus* which means wonderful. Healing is a wonderful and remarkable thing. Healing is happening all the time. We only need to open our awareness to experience the miracle of healing happening in and around us.

Healing is motion and change. We can see the wonder of healing every day. We can see it in the changes we make within ourselves. We can see it all around us in others. We are all attracted to the wonder of healing. We only need to be quiet so we can recognize the healing. Just as we must be still to hear a songbird, we need quiet to experience the flow of healing in this world.

When we accept things as they are and thereby allow things to change, we can relate to our world with amusement, compassion, forgiveness and neutrality. With acceptance, we create healing. Our spiritual perspective helps us have patience and allow the time it takes to create change in this physical world. We can then see the power that we have as spirit to create any change we need.

HEALING

Each of us has chosen to be here on this Earth. We are here to mature as spiritual beings in order to return whole to our Creator. The physical body exemplifies our spiritual passage here on Earth, in its birth, childhood, youth, adulthood, mature years and death. Each of these phases brings greater insight and maturity, in both the physical and spiritual journey. Just as we grow into maturity in a body, so must we grow into maturity as spirit. Our spiritual awareness and abilities grow in stages. If we were aware of all that is available for us at the beginning, we would be similar to a child with a bomb. We would have the power, without the wisdom to deal with it. Thus God reveals to us what we are ready to know as we grow through stages of opening awareness.

We choose to go through these steps as spirit to return to God as a mature aspect of the Cosmic Consciousness. In fact, we cannot fully return until we have reached spiritual maturity, as we would not have the wisdom and love to cope with such awareness and power. We put ourselves into the limits and seeming blindness of our physical world in order to get to know our own uniqueness by focusing on one lesson at a time. When we accept both our strengths and our weaknesses, we can heal ourselves, as we know our unique pattern. We have to learn to accept ourselves as we are and take total responsibility for our creativity. When we do accept ourselves as we are, we can grow and change. Self-acceptance brings healing.

Our choices during each life determine the experience we have on Earth. Freewill is necessary so we can actively choose to be a mature being and return of our own choice to God. We can return only when we are a whole and balanced entity, not divided by indecision or lack of commitment. We have to reach a state of total personal responsibility.

When we return to God, we must have our entire self to offer; any less is not acceptable. If we are unprepared at the end of a life phase, we simply return and continue to learn and grow, until we have reached our own level of balance and awareness. We all have the ability to heal ourselves and return to our Creator, as did the great teachers who have come to our planet to remind us who we are.

All of the great teachers, including Jesus Christ, Buddha, Mohammed, Lao Tsu, Moses and so many more, tell basically the same story. They all teach that we are part of the Divine Force manifesting in physical form. The great teachings portray the existence of God within man. They also teach us that we are able to communicate directly with God. They bring us the good news that we can be free of karma, or spiritual cycles, and can, through faith and forgiveness, completely return to God. It is as if we are asleep and their messages awaken us to the Divine plan.

The purpose of these teachers was to awaken us to our spiritual nature and our ability to heal ourselves so that we might attain this state of grace with the One God. These great teachers or messengers of God were all healers. They were healers because of their clear communication with God. They were able to have this level of communication because they continued to heal themselves. They were healing themselves to be able to serve God. They were able to act as a powerful force in the world by healing themselves and being a clear messenger of God.

HEALING

This planet is a place for us to learn and grow. Our goal is to allow the manifestation of the Godforce within each of us. It is ideally a place for us to mature spiritually by learning lessons as we manifest and create in physical form. Unfortunately, most have forgotten this and become lost in the physical aspect of this reality.

The greatest confusion about our spirituality comes when we attempt to explain or understand God and the spiritual realm through our physical concepts. We try to define God in physical terms and fill our image of God with emotions, ethics, needs and conflict. God is whole, complete and without conflict. The Cosmic Consciousness is without struggle, as God is in balance. We must heal ourselves to move toward this state of wholeness and harmony.

The purpose of our sojourn on this Earth is not to become the Earth or to be overwhelmed by it, but to use it creatively and lovingly to learn our lessons. We need to remember how to work with the physical reality of Earth, to nurture it and ourselves, in order to grow toward spiritual awareness through our life experiences. Unfortunately, we get caught in our limited perspectives and create pain, loneliness, doubt and death that keep us in fear. We allow the fear and doubt to keep us from our awareness of our Divine Inner Light.

It is possible for each of us to emerge into the awareness of light and re-establish both our joy in the Earth and our communication with God. This is where we need our healing skills and abilities. As we manifest spiritually in a body here on Earth, we discover what we have come here to learn and what we have come to teach. We have to discover what limits we created or accepted which we need to overcome. We have many self healing projects to complete in order to balance our energies and learn our lessons in any one life.

Each being has an inner journey to make to reawaken his spiritual awareness and meet the challenges chosen for learning. Each lifetime is unique, just as each soul is unique. We heal ourselves as we make mistakes, feel frustrations and strong emotions, experience pain and stumble along learning our lessons. Healing is a process that continues throughout our existence. The seeming difficulties are the opportunities for healing. The illness, problem or frustration is the physical sign that we as spirit need to balance or need to regain our spiritual perspective. Just as a child gets up after falling and continues to learn to walk, we have to keep healing ourselves to learn our lessons. When we pay attention to our creations and take responsibility for them, we heal ourselves.

As we balance our awareness of spirit and body, we realize that there is no "good" or "bad", only what is beneficial and what is not. We regain our harmony between spirit and body when we create the motion of healing. We learn that we are the ones creating our earthly experience and that we can change whatever we do not like. We realize that we can create in and through the body and we can also create and heal while outside of our physical body. The healing of conscious awake time and the healing of "dreams" are both powerful experiences. We are learning to work through and with the body, and its emotions and intellect, and outside of these limits as well.

HEALING

As the balancing act of healing continues, we learn that we receive what we give. We see that our choices create our experience and that we have the power to choose. Through healing we can begin to choose beneficial actions and thoughts, instead of ones which are programmed in and automatic. We can choose and project tolerance instead of judgement, and heal ourselves and all those around us.

Our healing continues as we start to balance our male and female aspects, such as our projection and reception of energies. We continue to balance our intellect and affection, and our wisdom and our love. All of these aspects of our spiritual and physical power can be brought into balance and harmony through our continued focus on self healing.

When we have healed ourselves and balanced our energies to a fine tune, we are ready to harmonize with all other things. The most exciting aspect of healing is its purpose and goal: to return to God.

Church of Divine Man
CDM Psychic Institute
2402 Summit Ave.
Everett, WA 98201
(206) 258-1449

Branch Locations

Bellingham CDM
1311 "I" St.
Bellingham, WA 98225
(206) 671-4291

Spokane CDM
N 2803 Lincoln
Spokane, WA 99205
(509) 325-5771

Portland CDM
3314 SW First Ave.
Portland, OR 97201
(503) 228-0740

Tacoma CDM
4604 N 38th
Tacoma, WA 98407
(206) 759-7460

Seattle CDM
2007 NW 61st St.
Seattle, WA 98107
(206) 782-3617

Vancouver BC CDM
P.O. Box 80412
Vancouver, BC V5H 3X6

If you are interested in learning more about healing and meditation, contact the Church of Divine Man/CDM Psychic Institute, or one of its Branches, for information.

Rt. Rev. Mary Ellen Flora lives, teaches and heals in the Pacific Northwest. Her enthusiasm for healing and change attract people from all walks of life in search of healing and information about healing. All who come receive validation that they are spirit and can heal themselves.

Mary Ellen brings a spiritual perspective to everything she does and to every encounter. This same perspective animates her work, and sheds fresh insight on the subjects she illuminates through her teaching and writing.

She and her husband, Rt. Rev. M. F. "Doc" Slusher, are co-founders and Bishops of the Church of Divine Man/CDM Psychic Institute, a Washington, Oregon and British Columbia organization based on spiritual freedom and growth. They bring a great deal of amusement, joy and fun to their work as to all aspects of life.

Prior to her work with the Church, Mary Ellen taught pre-kindergarten, high school, and was a Youth Program Director of the YMCA.